JOURNEY TOWARDS WORLD RECORDS

SWEET MEMORIES IN MY WORLD RECORD ATTEMPTS

SANJITH

Made with ❤ on the Notion Press Platform
www.notionpress.com

Contents

Acknowledgements

I would like to express my sincere gratitude to my Mother Aishwarya Bharathi and my Father K.R.S.Bharathi Kiruba for their love and affection. I would like to express my love and affection to my Grandparents Mr.K.R.Subramanian, Mrs.K.R.S.Lalitha, Mr.Mohan and Mrs.Brema I would like to express my special thanks to my school management and Principal Dr. Sunanda.C for the support and motivation she provides for all of us to exhibit our talents. I would like to thank our Head Mistress Priya Suresh Madam for her motivation and guidance. I would like to express my sincere thank to my class teachers Aneesh Fathima madam and Laishangbam Elina Devi madam for their guidance and support. I like to thank all my Teachers Karthika.M madam, Geetha.M madam, B.Rajkumar sir, M.Rajanandhini madam, Radhika madam, Leena Sidharthan madam, Vinod Sir, Saravanan sir for their support and guidance to me. I would like to express my sincere thanks to Jayasree madam for editing my work for the book.

CHAPTER ONE

About the author/ Narrator/Biographer

I am B.Sanjith, a nine year old boy studying Grade 4 in Nehru International School, Thirumalayampalam, Coimbatore. I learn music from the age of four and for me Music is the essence of soul and life. My Guru Mr. Sivagiri is teaching me keyboard for half a decade. I am proud to be a recipient of five World records so far. Three of which in music, another record for fastest puzzle solver and one in a group of people for a Guniess record. I love to play cricket and learn music with composing my own tunes. This is my first book and I feel excited and proud to share my thoughts on various aspects like music, journey of world records etc. I feel the readers like my book and expects your feedback for my improvements in future.This is B. Sanjith, a nine year old boy doing Grade 4 in Nehru International School, Thirumalayampalam, Coimbatore. I am learning music right from the age of four. According to me Music is the essence of soul and life. My Guru Mr. Sivagiri is teaching me keyboard for half a decade. I am glad to be a recipient of five World records so far. Out of five records three records for music, fourth record for fastest puzzle solver and the final one in a group of people for a Gunnies record. I am fond of spending my precious time in playing cricket and learning music by composing my own tunes. This is my first book and I feel excited and cheerful to share my profound thoughts on various aspects like music, journey of world records etc. I thought this book will make the readers to create a live image of my achievements. As a budding star I expects your valuable feedback for my improvements in future

B.Sanjith (9yr Old boy with 5 World Records)

CHAPTER TWO

My Exploration towards the World Record / A Journey towards the World Record

I am extremely delighted to hold Five Records even at this age. My First world Record was or fastest puzzle solving which I received at the age of "Seven". Solving puzzles and playing other indoor games were my passion. My parents spare their precious time at home with me. They used to play games, narrate stories and motivate my talents. As the days goes I am passionate towards puzzles and my parents gifted me with various puzzles to satisfy my likings and inspire me.

Once I was busy in solving puzzles my father noticed my way of solving the puzzle. He made way for my interests. And he said that it is very hard for others to solve these puzzles in short duration and he cheered up to do to my best. One day he came with surprise that he applied for the World Record as a Fastest Puzzle solver and the committee agreed to submit all the evidence and go ahead for the record. Due to pandemic, it was suggested that the record attempt should be made in school in front of the board members and Teachers with all 360 Degree camera recording with a authorized person for monitoring time.

Unfortunately, it was the initial stage of pandemic and people rarely comes out of their homes in India. Still when we requested my school for the attempt they happily agreed and took all needy steps for the record attempt. They facilitated all the necessary arrangements and I have solved the complicated puzzled within 2 Min: 31 Sec that was still considered as the World record so far. It was mainly happened only with the support of my school "Nehru International School". It could make my first World record dream.

The next passion was also noticed by my parents that was my interest on music especially in playing keyboard. I was learning Music for the past five years, my parents observed my skill in playing keyboard continuously without reading the notes. My parents encouraged me for continuous practice finally I could achieve my Second World Record in the field of music "Most played songs in keyboard as a Eight year old boy". After this I have got a couple of World records for music and I am certified as "Playing most songs in single hand in keyboard". The next title of mine was "Playing maximum patriotic songs for 76 min during the occasion of 76th Independent day". All these Worlds records on music which I want to submit as a gratitude for my beloved and my well-wisher Musical Guru Mr. Sivagiri as he was the one who thought me music right from the beginning and encourage me for my success. As a team it's a memorable journey of my participation in a Gunnies World Record attempt that took place during the Teacher's day celebration and I am proud that our team got recorded in the Guinness World record.

Some External Awards and Recognitions

CHAPTER THREE

Other Notorious Awards and Recognition

Apart from theses World records I have won several awards and prizes. I am glad share my other achievements. I have won the First Prize in the International Musical Event organized by "Krsto Tassel-Kidsup" in 2019. It was an online musical event because of the pandemic situation and I could perform my Keyboard musical performance for the event. I have received good comments from the Jury of the panel for my efforts and also the scope for improvements in the field of learning music. I am deeply excited when I got my first prize in International Musical Competition. Next I felt really happy by participating at "Star performer" in India which was a trending contest for several musical events and I have participated in the instrumental category.

Star Performer Award in INdian Level Musical contest

Independence Day Musical ceremony Award

Guiness Record Attempt with the team

CHAPTER FOUR

X [Stages Programs] My Stage Shows

I am highly delighted in sharing my about my stage performances that took place at various places. I am extremely delighted when I got the first opportunity to play in a musical event at Coimbatore. My Musical Guru gave the opportunity to participate in the event for the first time. I got the chance to perform in front of around 600 people. I was not nervous as my Guru was near to me and when I completed my session in music I have received applauds from the participants. Still, I remember many of them came to my parents stating that they want their kids to learn music. My parents were saying about my journey in music and guided them how their kids can start their musical journey by keeping as their model. I still believe many of my peer kids who came for the event might have joined the classes for music and I feel that was the real credit which I have received from the stage.

First Stage Performance

CHAPTER FIVE

Music from Nature

Nature is always the best mentor for me in my journey of music. Yes every day I learn music from different versions of our Mother Nature. My Mentor and musical Guru " Mr.Sivagiri" is teaching me various aspects of music in keyboard and vocal music and always I could relate it to the Nature who provokes me to take the essence of music from it. Music from rain can teach me the swaras. Morning sound of Coo coo resembles me the Raga "Abogi". When I travel I can relate the drizzling sound of air and the train to Raga "Malahari". All these gurus are helping my musical journey and I always believe music is the essence of my soul and nature is the soul of music. Whenever I visit any water fall I can relate the Raga "Sankarabaranam" with the beautiful sound of the flow of water flow. Whenever I decide to create my own tune first I think of my mother nature in various forms like rain, breeze, water flow, chirping sound of birds etc which triggers me various tunes. I feel I am the part of nature and nature is the real source of music. I wish the readers to explore our mother nature to the depth as our soul to learn and lead a happy and healthy life.

Wish all the readers the best !!!

Music from Beautiful Nature

CHAPTER SIX

About my Parents

I still remember the day when my parents were searching for music class across Coimbatore and other nearby cities. It was 22 rejections initially and for each rejection when they came out and said "Noissues, All for Goodness", the rejections are due to he needs to get a good Guru". They were not upset rather they tried every possible way and finally took me to my Musical Guru" Mr. Sivagiri". Still, I remember in the second class itself they were observing me from doors while I hardly played only 2 min for the keyboard which came to me in rotation. The moment they asked my Guru what the keyboard cost is and where it can be brought. Still remember they never gone to home post class rather they went to a musical shop and brought keyboard understanding its importance in initial days of learning itself. Still I remember the words of them "Music is God and Keyboard needs to be played as devotion to God". Still I only do my duty and its my parents who identifies all possible opportunities for me.

My Proud Parents

CHAPTER SEVEN

About my School and Teachers

I am studying at Nehru International School in the class 4A. It is my school and my Teachers encouragement, motivation and guidance which is the support for all my Five World Records. It is always a great and enjoy moments for me to go school very day meet my friends, learn from teachers, study , play and gather together. Really I feel the missing of school last year during the pandemic where I couldn't meet my friends, teachers in physical even thought we meet virtually every day. It is from my First class teacher " Anish madam" , I learnt the discipline and dedication. My present class teacher "Elina madam" is the one who thought us how to be motivated and structured for all our activities. I learnt the passion towards language from my Tamil teacher "---". I always try to learn passion towards people and disciplined work and team building by seeing and learning from my Head Misstress " Priya madam" I got the interest of becoming a Senior most person of an organization with good Management skill in future which got inspired from my Principal Mam "Dr.Sunantha Madam" seeing her administration and vision for the school.

Facilitation of World Record from my School and Management

CHAPTER EIGHT

About my Musical Guru

Mr.Sivagiri is my Musical Guru. Still I remember my parents saying when I was LKG they decided to put me up in any one of the musical instrument class. For the same they approached 22 Masters and every one of them rejected me stating I am too young and naughty boy. It was Sivagiri sir who saw me for a minute and understood I have some talent and definitely he is potential for Keyboard. Mr. Sivagiri teaches several types of instruments including Veena, Violin, Tabla, Drums, Flute etc The best part I like to my Master apart from his deep knowledge in music is his patience and understanding the kids interest and thoughts. He does not apply same technique to all students parallel rather he takes different approach and routes which ensures all of his students gets what he says as per their capability, knowledge, interest etc. It is finally I can proudly say all my friends, brothers, sisters of my Srutilaya musical school finally becomes a talented musician through his motivation, teaching and support. I like the most important part is the exposure and the stages we get through him with free of cost. He always takes us for any musical event happening in temples, special events etc which makes us an opportunity to be in a stage where several audience can see our talent as well as we gets confidence among our self. I would like to express my sincere gratitude to my Guru "Mr. Sivagiri" for all his love and passion for teaching which makes all of our fellow students to get deep knowledge and success in our musical career. I would like to submit all my World records in music to his feet as only with his teachings and mentoring I got the knowledge which I could perform proudly in the respective stages. I thank my almighty for showing me a great mentor for my musical journey which I believe I am gifted the most in this world.

With My Musical Guru Mr.SivaGiri

CHAPTER NINE

First Interview in Radio Channel

After getting fifth World record I was surprised to get a call from Radio Mirchi for an Interview. I was so excited to be inside the interview room and Mr. RJ Naveen took me the interview session. He was so patience to ask Questions and make me to speak properly as it was my first time to be in such a session. I still remember I was playful and he took efforts to make me speak. He was also playing like a Kid along with me and he completed the interview.

SANJITH

First Interview at Radio Mirchi

CHAPTER TEN

First Interview in Television channels

After getting these World records it was very happy that some news channels from Tamil Nadu and National Channels interviewed me along with my parents and telecasted in the channel. I still remember I felt shy while speaking but the reporters encourage me to speak and they hand holded me for topics which I try to explain. I felt very happy when I see myself in the television first time.

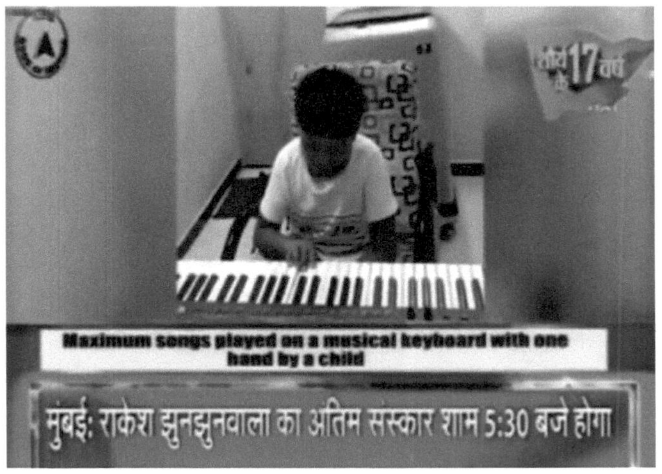

My First Television Interview

Printed by Libri Plureos GmbH in Hamburg,
Germany